Published by Eagle Publications
P O Box 73374, London W3 3FZ, England.
A Paperback Original

First published in the United Kingdom in 2020

Text copyright © 2020 Roselle Thompson

The right of Roselle Thompson to be identified as the Author
of this work has been asserted by her.

Cover design by V3Creative Designs

ISBN 978-1-8381068-1-2

A CIP catalogue record for this book is available from the British Library

All Rights Reserved

This book is sold subject to the condition that it shall not, by way of trade or otherwise, be lent, hired out or otherwise circulated in any form of binding or cover other than that in which it is published. No part of this publication may be reproduced, stored in a retrieval system, or transmitted in any form or by any means (electronic, mechanical, photocopying, recording or otherwise) without the prior written permission of Eagle Publications.

All paper used by Eagle Publications is SFI (Sustainable Forestry Initiative) and PEFC (Programme for the Endorsement of Forest Certification Schemes) Certified.

This is a work of fiction. Names, characters, incidents and dialogues are products of the author's imagination or are used fictitiously. Any resemblance to actual people, living or dead, events or locales is entirely coincidental.

Printed in the United Kingdom and United States by
Lightning Source for Eagle Publishers

www.eaglepublications.co.uk

EAGLE PUBLICATIONS

About this Book

This **Phonics & Spelling Workbook 1 is** designed to provide a more indepth study and practice in the *Phonic Sound structure*, with focus on the *Long vowel sounds*. The work is organized in a differentiated way, for ease of use in the classroom via three strategies – **FOCUS, EXTENSION AND CHALLENGE** which support the development of Phonics and Spellings skills in this book.

For example, each Long Vowel sound is presented with a <u>FOCUS</u> on developing and mastering each Sound presented. Then skills are further developed via <u>EXTENSION</u>, presented as intensive work, based on the sound pattern and rules provided. This enables practice and independent or group work, for greater understanding within the unit. Using this *Extension* strategy, students are encouraged to test their knowledge, by applying the skills learnt in the *Focus* exercises.

Then more intensive work is provided by the <u>CHALLENGE</u> exercises, which test the child's knowledge of the skills learnt in the unit. These are tasks for the student to both enjoy and do independently, in order to ensure competence of the work done; before a smooth progression onto the next sound pattern or Unit in this Workbook.

The approaches used in this **Phonics & Spelling Workbook 1** are tried and tested strategies used within the classroom, which have provided great success over many years.

A Certificate of Achievement is provided at the end of each Unit of Long Vowel Sound completed. This helps to track record of the skills learnt in assessment and to reward the child for the work done in each Unit.

Who is this book for?

All Primary years, especially those who already have an initial understanding of the Short Vowel Sound practice and now need to move on to more advanced spelling and understanding of the structure of the Long Vowel Sounds.

The books in this series are free-standing, so a child can work through each one or focus on the individual area of need. Moreover, it provides a comprehensive course in spelling and vocabulary development of the English Phonetic sound structure which enables greater indepth understanding of word-power development.

Whichever group a student belongs to, competence as well as confidence will grow.

The right of Roselle Thompson to be identified as the author of this work has been asserted by her in accordance with the Copyright, Designs & Patents Act 1988. All rights reserved. No part of this publication may be reproduced in any material form (including photocopying or storing it in any medium by electronic means and whether or not transiently or incidentally to some other use of this publication), without the written permission of the copyright owner, except in accordance with the provisions of the Copyright, Designs & Patents Act 1988. Applications for the copyright owner's written permission to reproduce any part of this publication should be addressed to the publisher –Eagle Publications. **Warning.** The doing of an unauthorized act in relation to this copyright work, may result in court action as a claim for damages and criminal prosecution.

Published by: Eagle Publications   ISNB 978-1-8381068-1-2   (c) Roselle Thompson 2020

Phoenix Study Guides

PHONICS & SPELLING WORKBOOK 2

By

Roselle Thompson

This Book Belongs to:

Name: ....

EAGLE PUBLICATIONS

CONTENTS PAGE

Page	Phonic Letter Patterns	Focus Page No.	Extension Page No.	Challenge Page No.
	LONG *a* PHONIC SOUNDS			
1.	a_e letter pattern	1	4	5
6.	ay letter pattern	6	8	9
10.	ai letter pattern	10	12	13
14.	ey letter pattern	14	15	15
17.	ea letter pattern	17	18	18
19.	ei letter pattern	19	20	20
21.	eigh letter pattern	21	22	24
25.	Review of *Long A* letter patterns			
26.	Certificate of Achievement			
	Long *e* PHONIC SOUNDS			
27.	ee letter pattern	27	30	31
34.	e_e letter pattern	34	35	36
37.	ey letter pattern	37	38	39
40.	y letter pattern	40	42	43
44.	ea letter pattern	44	46	47
48.	ei letter pattern	48	49	50
52.	ie letter pattern	52	53	54
55.	Review of *Long E* letter patterns			
57.	Certificate of Achievement			
58.	High Frequency Words List			

LONG A - PHONIC SOUND PRACTICE

FOCUS

DO YOU REMEMBER the list of **Long a** sounds?

Here are the different ways we can write *Long a* sound:

Sounds like the letter a (a_e/)		Sounds like the letter a (ay/ai/eigh/ey/ea)	
lake	bake	rain	snail
hate	rake	weigh	holiday
date	plate	stay	delay
make	pale	wait	may
skate	sale	mail	beige
take	pane	prey	great
state	mane	play	maid
gate	age	tail	train
safe	face	paid	grey

In this Workbook, we will begin by practising the different ways of saying and writing the *Long A* sounds.

From the box above you will see there are 6 different ways. Let's practise them to make both your reading and spelling easier, as you move on to the next stages in your learning.

Your practice will be to look at each Long sound separately as follows:

1.	a_e
2.	ay
3.	ai
4.	ey
5.	ea
6	eigh

A Certificate of Achievement is provided at the end of the *Long A* Unit to reward you for your heard work in completing all the *Long A* sounds successfully. Happy learning!

Long a Sound Practice with a_e pattern

LET'S PRACTICE THE a_e PATTERN OF WRITING AND SAYING THE *LONG A* SOUND:

When a_e is written like this, it's called a split digraph: a digraph is when two vowel letters next to each other make one sound. When they are separated by a consonant, (a letter that is not a vowel), we call it a split digraph. For example, in this word:

m a k e - we say the a_e sounds together.

This is because the a has a helper vowel e, at the end of the word, (sometimes called *magic e* or *silent e*): It gives the two letters the name a.

Sounding them separately, m-a-k-e will <u>NOT</u> give you the LONG *A* SOUND

You must do this - m a k e

Now Practice saying the sound of the words in the box below:

Sounds like the letter a (a_e)	
lake	bake
snake	rake
date	plate
make	pale
skate	sale
take	plane
cake	mane
gate	age
safe	face

(c) 2020 Roselle Thompson   Phonic & Spelling Workbook 2

From the box above write the word that's linked to these pictures

....

....

....

....

....

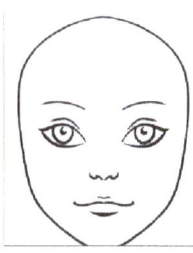
....

....

....

....

....

....

EXTENSION

NOW READ THESE SENTENCES WITH *LONG A,* AND CIRCLE *LONG A* WORDS

1.	There were many boats on the l**ake**.
2.	Look at her f**ace**.
3.	The children are making a c**ake**.
4.	Look at her f**ace**.
5.	John will t**ake** the school bus today.
6.	The window p**ane** is wet.
7.	Please t**ake** the bus to school.
8.	A cat c**ame** to my house today.
9.	Let's get a new dress from the s**ale**.
10.	Please stand at the main g**ate**.
11.	Let's go and sit by the l**ake**.
12.	Mum said, "You are l**ate**!"
13.	He is waiting at the main g**ate**.
14.	What is his **age**?
15.	I made a big mist**ake**.

CHALLENGE

Find the a_e words in each line and circle them.
(The first one has been done for you)

1.	rain map male ship *mane* fall
2.	say age may shy pale come
3.	state hay safe pay tried play
4.	late dear lane more give ate
5.	saw pain same took name maid

Match the words that have the a_e sound pattern in them

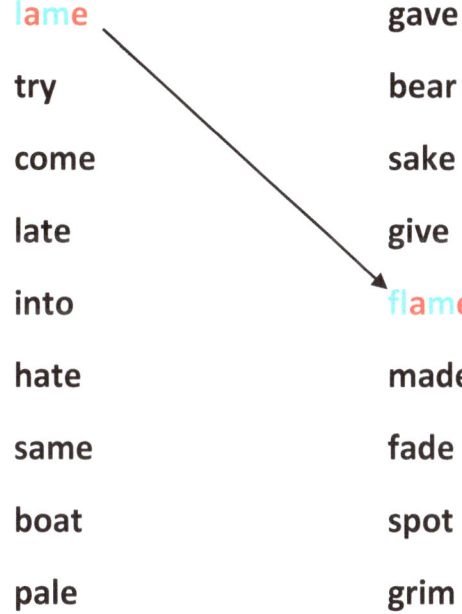

lame — flame
try
come
late
into
hate
same
boot
pale

gave
bear
sake
give
made
fade
spot
grim

Now WRITE your favourite a_e word here...

Draw a picture to do with the word face

Long a Sound Practice with ay pattern

Sounds like the letter a	with the *(ay)* pattern
say	lay
day	bay
delay	hay
may	pay
pay	ray
today	way
pray	clay
tray	stay
spray	slay
play	okay

We now move on to another sound letter pattern **ay**.

The **ay** sound pattern just has one sound, just like the *a_e* that you practised before.

The two letters (**ay**) together give the long sound of **a**.

For example: d-ay

Now practice saying the sound of words in the word-box above.

Here are some Pictures, write the words for them, using the word-box above.

....

....

  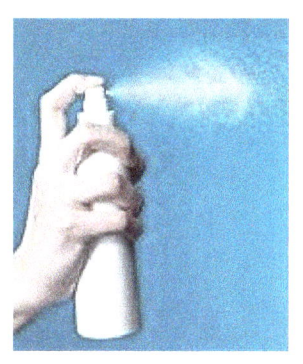

....

....

Draw a picture of a sunny day here:

EXTENSION

FIRST READ THESE SENTENCES WITH AY SOUNDING WORDS AND THEN CIRCLE THEM.

THEN WRITE the sentences

1.	It is a hot day.
2.	Tom may come to school.
3.	The man gave hay to his cows.
4.	I will make a cake for you today.
5.	Let me have your tray.
6.	It is Sunday today.
7.	Stay here till mum comes.
8.	I will pay for the eggs.
9.	Come and play with me he said.
10.	Let us pray with you.

CHALLENGE

FIND THE WORD THAT DOES NOT BELONG
(The first one has been done for you)

1.	joy may got hot trot sob hob
2.	spray play way came ray hay
3.	sit pin pig hit play in tip pip
4.	lot not mop okay got hob rob
5.	bray clay slay stay spray fake

Match the words that have ay sound pattern in them

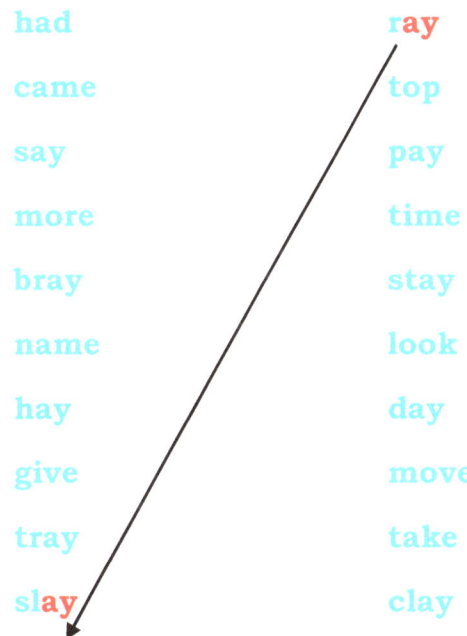

had   ray
came   top
say   pay
more   time
bray   stay
name   look
hay   day
give   move
tray   take
slay   clay

Write your favourite ay word here……………………………..

Draw a picture here to do with the word PLAY

FOCUS

Long a Sound Practice with ai pattern

Sounds like the letter a (ai)	
rain	snail
mail	chain
tail	main
wait	paid
mail	laid
pail	grain
train	maid
pain	rail
paid	afraid

Let continue with *Long a sound* but with another sound letter pattern - **ai.**
The **ai** sound pattern just has one sound, just like the **ay** pattern that you practised before. The two letters (**ai**) together give the long sound of **a**.

For example: t-ai-l

Now practice saying the sound of words in the word-box above.

Here are some Pictures, write the words for them, using the word-box above.

....

....

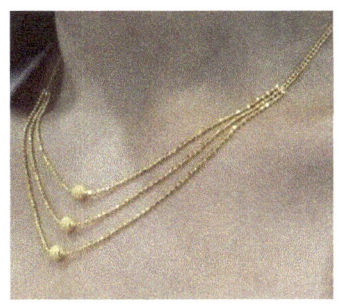

....

....

....

(c) 2020 Roselle Thompson   *Phonic & Spelling Workbook 2*

EXTENSION

READ THESE SENTENCES WITH ai SOUNDING WORDS AND THEN CIRCLE THEM.   NOW WRITE the sentences

1.	The dog has a long tail.
2.	I paid for the milk.
3.	Let's play in the rain.
4.	We need to wait here for the train.
5.	I have a pain in my leg.
6.	The ship has a sail.
7.	I got a gold chain for my birthday.
8.	Meg the hen laid ten eggs.
9.	A maid cleaned the Queen's bedroom.
10.	Ben is not really afraid of the dark.
11.	Tom will fix the chain on his bike.
12.	The water went down the drain.
13.	She hit the nail with the hammer.
14.	The main door is locked.
15.	Do not wait at the bus stop.

How many sentences did you read correctly all by yourself?

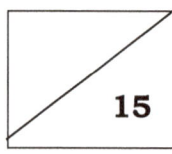

CHALLENGE

FIND THE WORD THAT DOES NOT BELONG
(The first one has been done for you)

1.	plain rail snail give main aid
2.	pray grain way say ray hay
3.	sat pan hail pay day tap pad
4.	vain trail fail paid weep hail rain
5.	fake spray slay mail clay bray

Match the words that have ai sound pattern in them

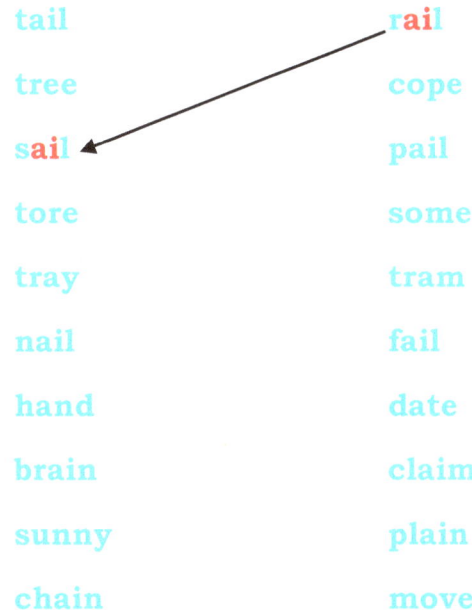

tail	rail
tree	cope
sail	pail
tore	some
tray	tram
nail	fail
hand	date
brain	claim
sunny	plain
chain	move

WORD SEARCH: See if you can find these words:

WAIT, TAIL, MAIL, TRAIN, RAIN

R	W	A	I	T
M	A	I	L	A
A	I	R	T	N
I	T	A	I	L
T	R	A	I	N

(c) 2020 Roselle Thompson   Phonic & Spelling Workbook 2

FOCUS

Long a Sound Practice with ey pattern

Sounds like the letter a (ey)
they
obey
prey
grey
hey

Let continue with *Long a sound* but with another sound letter pattern - **ey.** The **ey** sound pattern just has one sound, just like the *ai* pattern that you practised before. The two letters (**ey**) together give the long sound of **a**. You will notice that there are fewer words with the **ey** ending as *long a* sound.

For example: th-ey

Now practice saying the sound of words in the word-box above.

Here are some Pictures, write the words for them, using the word-box above.

   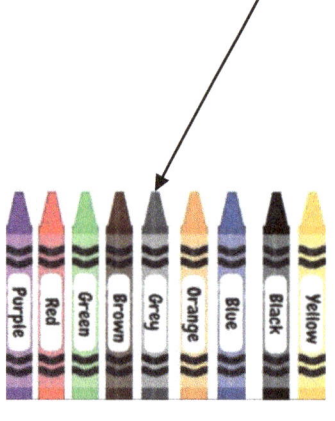   

....

EXTENSION

READ THESE SENTENCES WITH ey SOUND WORDS AND THEN CIRCLE THEM.

THEN WRITE the sentences

1.	They are coming to my house today
2.	Mum said that we need to obey her.
3.	Hey you! Come here! He shouted.
4.	Will they be coming to my party?
5.	The sky looks grey, it will rain.
6.	I need grey paint for my picture.
7.	The little deer is a prey for the lion.
8.	Dad will paint my room grey.
9.	Here they are, hiding behind the curtains!

CHALLENGE

FIND THE WORD THAT DOES NOT BELONG
(The first one has been done for you)

1.	play	way	they	hay	spray	bray
2.	pram	grey	save	sat	rat	may
3.	sail	pail	hail	obey	mail	tail	trail
4.	gate	fate	bake	rake	hey	hate	rate
5.	prey	spray	slave	mate	clay	brat

Match the words that have ey sound pattern in them

grain	grey
hard	tail
mate	prey
date	sail
obey	same
gate	rake
they	have
hey ⟶	convey

Write your favourite ey word here………………………………………

Draw a picture here to do with the word they

FOCUS

Long a Sound Practice With ea pattern

Sounds like the letter a (ea)
great
break
steak

Surprise, Surprise! Not many ea words with the long a sound! It's because this pattern is more popular in a different long sound. We will look at this interesting fact later in our workbook, but for now, let's look at the few ea pattern *long a* sounding words.

For example: **gr-ea-t**

Now practice saying the sound of the words in the word-box above.

Here are some Pictures, write the words for them, using the word-box above.

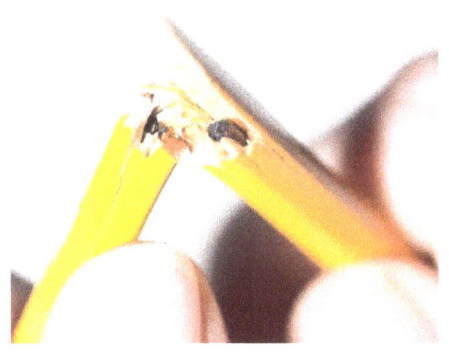 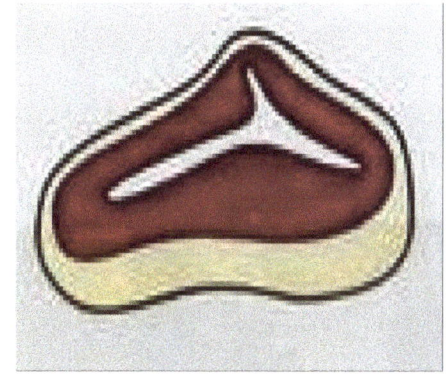

....

(c) 2020 Roselle Thompson   *Phonic & Spelling Workbook 2*

EXTENSION

READ THESE SENTENCES WITH ea SOUNDING WORDS LIKE a AND THEN CIRCLE THEM. THEN WRITE the sentences

1.	This is a great picture!
2.	Let us take a break said Tom.
3.	Did you break my pencil? he asked.
4.	Dad wants to have steak and chips for dinner.
5.	It is break-time said my teacher.
6.	This story sounds great, he said.

CHALLENGE

WORD SEARCH: See if you can find these words:

GREAT, BREAK, STEAK

S	T	B	A	K
B	E	R	A	T
G	R	E	A	T
B	T	A	R	B
S	T	K	A	K

Write your favourite ea word......................................

==FOCUS==

Long a Sound Practice with ei pattern

Sounds like the letter a (ei)
rein
vein
veil
beige
reign

Let continue with *Long a sound* but with another sound letter pattern - **ei.** The **ei** sound pattern just has one sound, just like the ea pattern that you practised before. The two letters (ei) together give the long sound of a.

For example: v-ei-l

Now practice saying the sound of words in the word-box above.

Here are some Pictures, write the words for them, using the word-box above.

      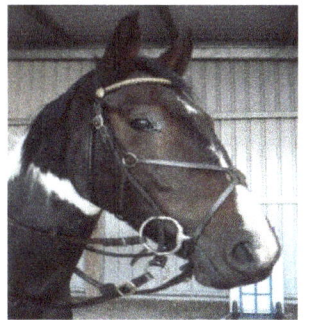

....

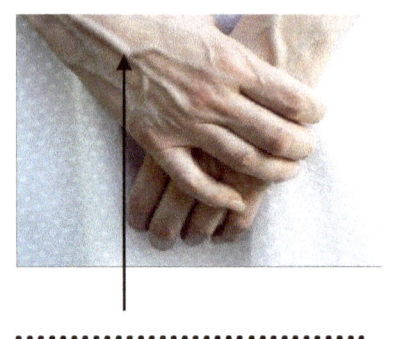 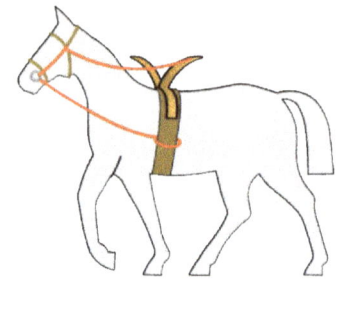 

....

EXTENSION

READ THESE SENTENCES WITH ei SOUNDING WORDS LIKE a AND THEN CIRCLE THEM.   THEN WRITE the sentences

1.	She wears a v**ei**l over her face.
2.	Can you see a v**ei**n in her hand?
3.	The Queen has r**ei**gned for 60 years.
4.	Hold on to the r**ei**ns of the horse.
5.	I want the walls in my room to be a b**ei**ge colour.
6.	The next person to r**ei**gn after the Queen will be Prince Charles.
7.	The wall in my classroom is painted b**ei**ge.
8.	Pam wore a b**ei**ge dress to my party.

CHALLENGE

WORD SEARCH: See if you can find these words:

REIN, VEIN, BEIGE, VEIL

B	E	V	R	B
E	R	E	G	E
V	E	I	N	I
G	I	L	B	G
E	N	G	E	E

FOCUS

Long a Sound Practice with eigh pattern

Sounds like the letter a (eigh)
eight
eighteen
weigh
weight
neigh
neighbour
eighty

Let continue with *long a sound* but with another sound letter pattern - **eigh**. The **eigh** sound pattern just has one sound, just like the **ei** pattern that you practised before. The four letters (**eigh**) together give the long sound of **a**.

For example: **n-eigh**

Now practice saying the sound of words in the word-box above.

Here are some Pictures, write the words for them, using the word-box above.

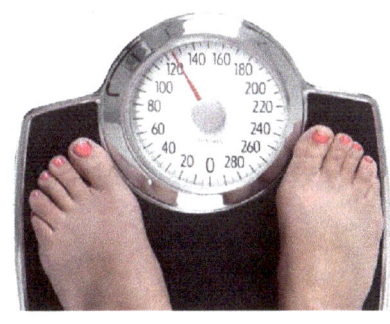

....

....

(c) 2020 Roselle Thompson Phonic & Spelling Workbook 2

....

....

EXTENSION

NOW READ THESE SENTENCES WITH eigh SOUNDING WORDS LIKE a AND THEN CIRCLE THEM.   THEN WRITE the sentences

1.	Sally is eight years old today.
2.	My brother is going to be eighteen years next year.
3.	Dad always weighs himself on our scale.
4.	A nurse weighs the babies on a scale.
5.	I have eighteen pencils in my bag.
6.	Our neighbour is very kind.
7.	He will be eighty years next week.
8.	Horses neigh, that is the sound they make.

NOW YOU NEED TO PRACTICE READING ALL THE *LONG A* SOUNDS

MIXED PRACTICE OF THE PATTERNS (a_e, ay, ai, ey, ea, eigh)

1.	I may go to the shop today.
2.	Can you say this word?
3.	This bed is on sale.
4.	What is the date today?
5.	Hold on to the horse's reins.
6.	He has a grey pencil.
7.	What is your weight?
8.	How much do you weigh?
9.	She has a pain in her leg.
10.	Get the mail from the post man.
11.	Let us play in the rain.
12.	I am going on holiday.
13.	This is great story.
14.	I am going on a train today.
15.	They are coming to my house.
16.	I am going to bake a cake today

How many sentences did you read correctly all by yourself?

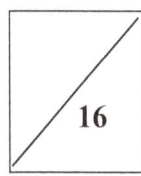

CHALLENGE

Match the words that have eigh sound pattern in them

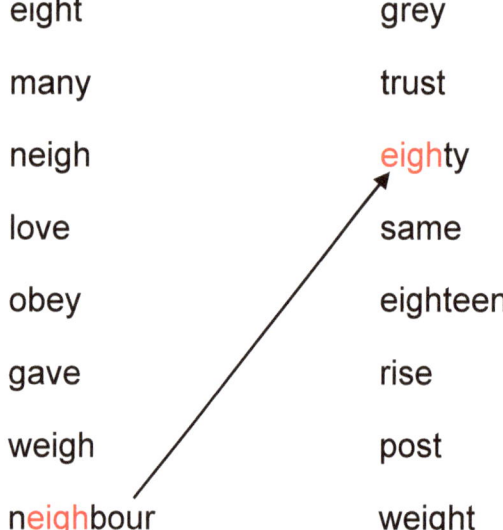

eight	grey
many	trust
neigh	eighty
love	same
obey	eighteen
gave	rise
weigh	post
neighbour	weight

WORD SEARCH: See if you can find these words:
NEIGH, WEIGH, EIGHTY, WEIGHT

N	O	N	E	V
E	W	E	I	E
W	E	I	G	H
H	I	G	H	I
T	G	H	T	G
Y	H	E	Y	W
S	T	V	R	S

Draw a picture of a cake and put **8 candles** on it

REVIEW ALL LONG A SOUNDS

> NOW TALK ABOUT THE DIFFERENT LONG *A* SOUND PATTERNS AGAIN. SEE IF YOU CAN WRITE THE WORDS FOR THESE PICTURES ALL BY YOURSELF

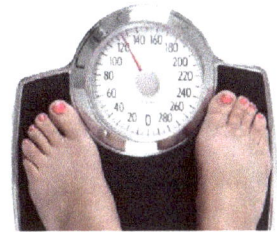

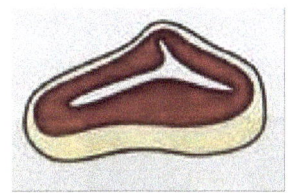

(c) 2020 Roselle Thompson *Phonic & Spelling Workbook 2*

CERTIFICATE OF ACHIEVEMENT

LONG A PHONIC SOUND PATTERNS

This Certificate is presented to:

………………………………………………………………………for successfully completing the entire LONG A SOUND PATTERNS as follows:

	I KNOW ALL MY a SOUND PATTERNS	
1.	a_e	✓
2.	ay	✓
3.	ai	✓
4.	ey	✓
5.	ea	✓
6.	eigh	✓

Comment: ……………………………………………………………………………

………………………………………………………………………………………………

………………………………………………………………………………………………

Teacher/Parent Signature: ……………………………………………………

Date: ……………………………………………………………………………………

LONG E - PHONIC SOUND PRACTICE

LET'S LOOK AT ANOTHER LONG SOUND – THIS TIME IT'S THE LONG E SOUND.

DO YOU REMEMBER the list of Long e sounds?
Here are the different ways we can write Long e sound:

Sounds like the letter (e) (y/i/ea/ei/ie)		Sounds like the letter (e) (e/ee/e_e/ey)	
mummy	reason	me	these
happy	eat	deep	complete
taxi	reach	been	secrete
heat	mean	need	extreme
mean	read	keep	money
tummy	meat	feed	alley
silly	peach	wheel	valley
treat	reach	be	turkey
bully	beat	teeth	kidney
teach	bleach	tree	greet
seat	funny	seem	donkey

We will now begin by practising the different ways of saying and writing the Long E sounds. We will practice 7 different ways to saying and writing Long e sound. Knowing them well will make both your reading and spelling easier, as you move on to the next stages in your learning. Your practice in this Workbook will be to look at each of the Long sounds separately as follows:

1.	ee
2.	e_e
3.	ey
4.	y
5.	ea
6.	ei
7.	ie

A Certificate of Achievement is provided at the end of the Long E Unit to reward you for your heard work in completing all the Long E sounds successfully. Happy learning!

Long e Sound Practice with ee pattern

PRACTICE THE ee PATTERN OF WRITING AND SAY THE *LONG E* SOUND:

The ee sound pattern just has one sound. The two letters (ee) together give the long sound of e.

For example: been

Sounds like the letter e (ee)	
been	deep
deep	knee
see	need
need	keep
teeth	seem
seeds	meet
free	feed
sweets	queen
wheel	tree

Now practice saying the sound of words in the word-box above.

See if you can write the words for these pictures

   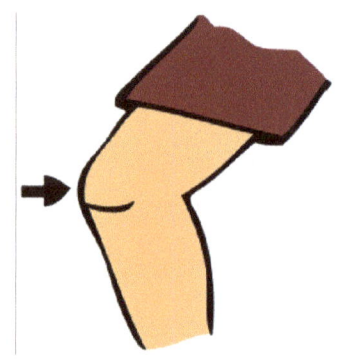

....

(c) 2020 Roselle Thompson Phonic & Spelling Workbook 2

Here are some Pictures, write the words for them, using the word-box above.

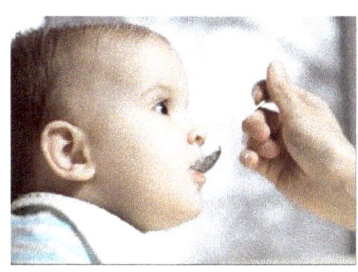

....

  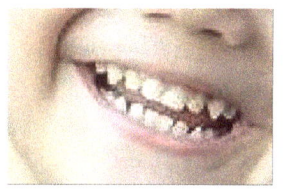

....

 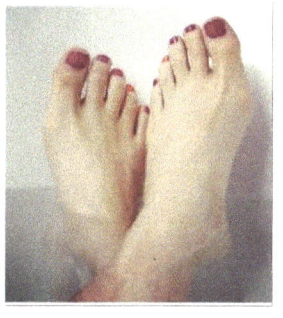

....

EXTENSION

NOW READ THESE SENTENCES WITH ee SOUND WORDS AND THEN CIRCLE THEM. THEN WRITE THE SENTENCES.

1.	Have you been to the shop?
2.	The water is deep.
3.	Can you see me?
4.	I can't see the mail.
5.	I need to go to the shop.
6.	Can you keep this for me?
7.	I can brush my teeth.
8.	It doesn't seem like rain.
9.	Here are some seeds.
10.	Let us meet at the bus stop.
11.	Will you be free at lunch time?
12.	Let us feed the ducks in the pond.
13.	I am going to buy some sweets.
14.	Mum doesn't like sweet coffee.
15.	She needs a wheel for her bike.

How many sentences did you read by yourself? / 15

CHALLENGE

Draw a picture about your favourite ee word

Match the words that have ee sound pattern in them

deep	read
duck	seen
green	many
rain	coffee
meet	been
weep	rain
said	need

WORD SEARCH: See if you can find these words:

MEET, SEED, TREE, AGREE, BEE
SEE, TEETH, SWEETS, WHEEL, KEEP

M	K	E	E	P	A
E	W	S	O	T	G
E	H	W	R	A	R
T	E	E	T	H	E
B	E	E	S	E	E
G	L	T	R	E	E
W	O	S	E	E	D

(2). MORE CHALLENGE: with *Long e* – with *ee* pattern

NOW WRITE A SENTENCE OF YOUR OWN WITH THESE WORDS.

1.	Need
2.	Sweet
3.	Been
4.	Seen
5.	Feet
6.	Meet
7.	Seed
8.	Free
9.	Teeth
10.	See
11.	Deep
12.	Wheel

(3). **MORE CHALENGE** - PRACTICE WITH ee PATTERN

| Meet | need | sweet | been | seen | feet | queen |
| seed | free | teeth | see | deep | wheel | tree | sleep |

Use the words in the box to put in the gaps.

1. This coffee is very...

2. I will.. you later.

3. Have you ....to work?

4. I will plant a ....in the ground.

5. Look at my ....I just brushed them.

6. The water in the pool is very..

7. I want to .... with you today.

8. The ....in my bike is broken.

9. Have you ....the Queen?

10. I ....to go to sleep now.

11. There is pain in my..

12. We can meet after work, when you are..

13. There is a .... in my garden.

14. There is a ....in England.

15. It's time for bed, let us go to..

How many sentences did you read by yourself?

/15

Long e Sound Practice with e_e pattern

Sounds like the letter e (e_e)
these
theme
eve
even
delete
scene
gene
compete
complete

Let continue with *Long e sound* but with another sound letter pattern – e_e. The e_e sound pattern just has one sound, just like the ee pattern that you practised before. The two letters (e_e) are a split digraph. Together give the long sound of e.

For example: these

Now practice saying the sound of words in the word-box above.

Here are some Pictures, write the words for them, using the word-box above.

....

(c) 2020 Roselle Thompson   Phonic & Spelling Workbook 2

....

....

:large_orange_diamond: EXTENSION

NOW READ THESE SENTENCES WITH e_e SOUND WORDS AND THEN CIRCLE THEM. THEN WRITE THE SENTENCES.

1.	He is not working this evening.
2.	Can you see the even numbers on the board?
3.	I want to delete this work and do it again.
4.	I am going to compete in the race.
5.	I wonder what's in these boxes.
6.	There is a funny scene in this cartoon.
7.	Jane's party is going to have a princess theme.

CHALLENGE

Match the words that have e_e sound pattern in them

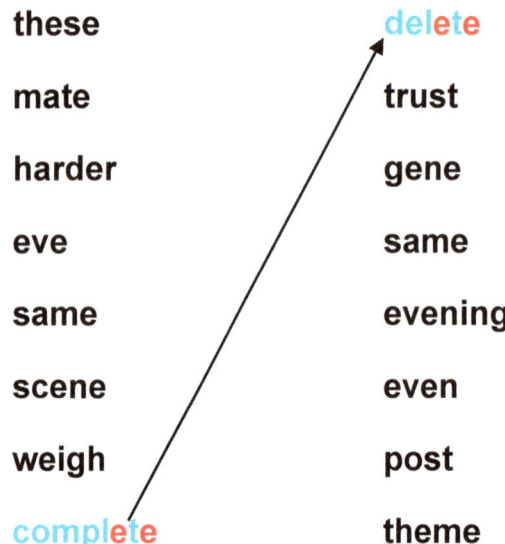

these   delete

mate   trust

harder   gene

eve   same

same   evening

scene   even

weigh   post

complete   theme

WORD SEARCH: See if you can find these words:

EVEN, GENES, EVE, SCENE, THESE

T	H	E	S	E
G	E	N	E	S
E	V	E	N	T
E	N	E	C	S

Draw a picture of an **even** number

FOCUS

Long e Sound Practice with ey pattern

Sounds like the letter e (ey)
key
monkey
money
donkey
valley
turkey
kidney
alley

Let continue with *Long e sound* but with another sound letter pattern – **ey**. The **ey** sound pattern just has one sound, just like the **e_e** pattern that you practised before. The two letters (**ey**) together give the long sound of **e**.

For example: mon ey

Now practice saying the sound of words in the word-box above.

Here are some Pictures, write the words for them, using the word-box above.

....

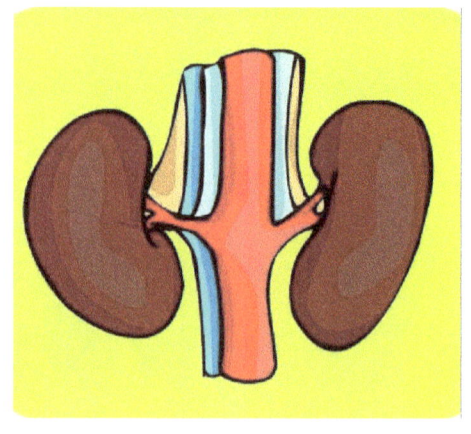

....

....

EXTENSION

NOW READ THESE SENTENCES WITH ey SOUND WORDS AND THEN CIRCLE THEM. THEN WRITE THE SENTENCES.

1.	Dad gave me some money to buy sweets.
2.	Some people have turkey for dinner at Christmas.
3.	I have a key for my room.
4.	The farmer has a donkey as well as a horse.
5.	This monkey likes bananas.
6.	The valley is between two mountains.
7.	We have kidneys in your body.

CHALLENGE

Match the words that have **ey** sound pattern in them

key	valley
marker	match
monkey	goat
evening	donkey
post	vast
kidney	even
weigh	turkey
gate	theme

WORD SEARCH: See if you can find these words:

KEY, KIDNEY, VALLEY, DONKEY, TURKEY, MONEY

Y	E	K	R	U	T
E	M	O	N	E	Y
K	I	D	N	E	Y
Y	E	L	L	A	V
D	O	N	K	E	Y

Draw a Picture of your favourite **ey** word

FOCUS

Long e Sound Practice with y pattern

Sounds like the letter e - (y)		
mummy	bunny	leafy
happy	hurry	pretty
tummy	sandy	party
silly	very	only
bully	stinky	scary
funny	cheeky	many
hungry	easy	family
every	greedy	icy
fairy	city	

Let continue with *Long e sound* but with another sound letter pattern – **y.**

The **y** sound pattern just has one sound; just like the **ey** pattern that you practised before. This **y** letter gives the long sound of **e.**

For example: happy

Now practice saying the sound of words in the word-box above.

Here are some Pictures, write the words for them, using the word-box above.

....

(c) 2020 Roselle Thompson   Phonic & Spelling Workbook 2

....

....

 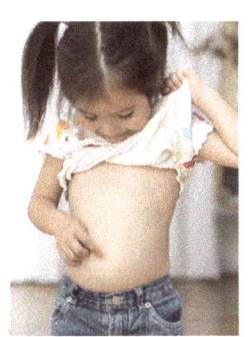 

....

....

EXTENSION

NOW READ THESE SENTENCES WITH y SOUND WORDS AND THEN CIRCLE THEM. THEN WRITE THE SENTENCES.

1.	I am very happy to meet you.
2.	Let us hurry or we will be late.
3.	Tom says that his hungry, he needs to eat.
4.	"Don't be silly," said Dad.
5.	This family is very big but mine is not.
6.	That white bunny is very furry and soft.
7.	We live in the city where it's noisy and busy.
8.	I have many friends in my school.
9.	One glass is full of milk but the other one is empty.
10.	I am going to have a party for my birthday.
11.	I like reading fairy tales, they are great.
12.	This work is easy for me, said Salim.
13.	Your dress is very pretty, where did you buy it from?
14.	We go to school every day.
15.	There was only one dog in the park today.

How many sentences did you read by yourself?

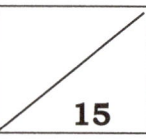

CHALLENGE

Match the words that have y sound pattern in them

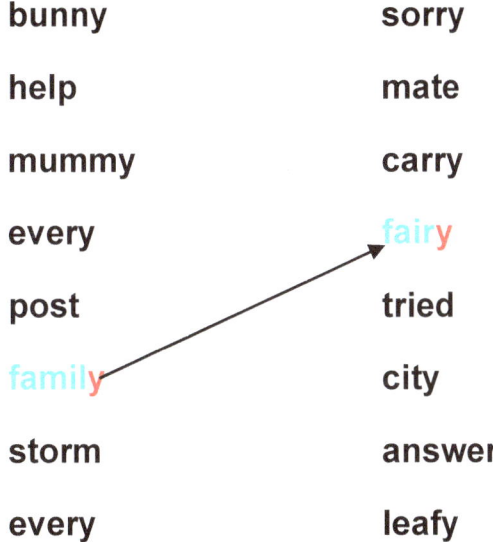

bunny	sorry
help	mate
mummy	carry
every	fairy
post	tried
family	city
storm	answer
every	leafy

WORD SEARCH: See if you can find these words:

EVERY, CITY, FAIRY, ICY, SILLY, ONLY, VERY, EASY,

O	B	E	A	S	Y
N	S	V	E	R	Y
L	V	E	M	O	A
Y	Y	R	I	A	F
I	C	Y	T	I	C
S	I	L	L	Y	P

Draw a Picture of your favourite y word

FOCUS

Long e Sound Practice with ea pattern

Sounds like the letter e - (ea)		
leaf	east	pea
beans	beak	heat
tea	cheap	leap
eat	clean	lead
team	cream	eagle
seat	dream	beam
meat	deal	please
meal	beat	sea
read	teach	meat

Let continue with *long e sound* but with another sound letter pattern – **ea.**

The **ea** sound pattern just has one sound; just like the **y** pattern that you practised before. The two letters (**ea**) together give the long sound of **e**.

For example:

Now practice saying the sound of words in the word-box above.

Here are some Pictures, write the words for them, using the word-box above.

....

(c) 2020 Roselle Thompson   Phonic & Spelling Workbook 2

....

....

....

....

EXTENSION

NOW READ THESE SENTENCES WITH ea SOUND WORDS AND THEN CIRCLE THEM. THEN WRITE THE SENTENCES.

1.	"I am going to eat pizza for lunch," said Tom.
2.	Do you want to play in our football team?
3.	The baby is sitting in his car seat.
4.	Some people do not eat meat.
5.	I wil teach you how to read, said my teacher.
6.	"Do you like beans?" She asked.
7.	Can you help me clean the class, please?
8.	I will lead and you will follow.
9.	I like cream with my strawberries.
10.	There is a ship on the sea.
11.	"These flowers are not real," she said.
12.	Mum likes to drink tea every day.
13.	The sun rises in the east each day.
14.	Let us have fish and chips for our meal, said John.
15.	The eagle flies very high up in the sky.

CHALLENGE

Match the words that have ea sound pattern in them

real	heat
send	hold
please	goat
windy	seat
every	easy
cheap	———→ lead
sweets	dream
read	learn

WORD SEARCH: See if you can find these words:

SEA, EAGLE, EAT, MEAT, TEA, TEAM, PEA, BEAMS, DREAM, HEAT, SEAL, PEAT

D	R	E	A	M	B
E	S	E	A	L	E
L	H	A	P	E	A
G	E	T	E	A	M
A	A	M	T	D	S
E	T	L	A	E	R

Draw a Picture of your favourite ea word

FOCUS

Long e Sound Practice with ei pattern

Sounds like the letter e - (ei)

receive
either
being
seize
leisure
ceiling
deceive
receipt

Let continue with *Long e sound* but with another sound letter pattern – **ei.**
The **ei** sound pattern just has one sound; just like the **ea** pattern that you practised before. The two letters (**ei**) together give the long sound of **e.**

For example: being
Now practice saying the sound of words in the word-box above.

Here are some Pictures, write the words for them, using the word-box above.

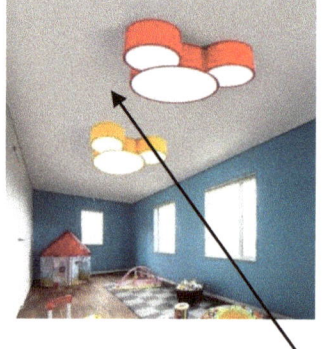

....

....

....

EXTENSION

NOW READ THESE SENTENCES WITH ei SOUND WORDS AND THEN CIRCLE THEM. THEN WRITE THE SENTENCES.

1.	Pat will receive a present from her sister on her birthday.
2.	Which sweet do you want, either this one or that one?
3.	It's not fair; he always deceives others when he plays.
4.	I play games on my laptop when it is my leisure time.
5.	Mum took the receipt from the shop-keeper.
6.	That red baloon is up high on my ceiling.
7.	We will either go to the zoo visit friends today.

8.	My baby brother is being noisy, he is crying again!
9.	The police will seize him; he put things in his bag he had not paid for.
10.	When it's our leisure time, I read and mum listens to music.

CHALLENGE

Match the words that have **ei** sound pattern in them

either	being
mask	things
receive	deceive
music	fire
just	leisure
neither	enable
pocket	receipt
seize	market

WORD SEARCH: See if you can find these words:

EITHER, DECEIVE, RECEIVE,
CEILING, EITHER, LEISURE, RECEIPT

C	E	L	R	R	D
E	I	E	E	E	E
I	T	I	C	C	C
L	H	S	E	E	E
I	E	U	I	I	I
N	R	R	P	V	V
G	A	E	T	E	E

MORE CHALENGE

Write your favourite ei **word here..and then draw a picture about it.**

Complete the sentences below with words from this box.

receive	either	being	seize
leisure	ceiling	deceive	receipt

1. I was given a ....when I paid for my sweets.
2. Mum says that I can have either a cake or an apple.
3. The bully............................the girl's pencil and ran away.
4. Did you ....a letter from your Nan?
5. I am ....very quiet because I'm in the library.
6. I go swimming when I have............................ time.
7. He tried to ....his friend when he played the game.
8. There is a balloon on my ....and it's too high for me to get it.

FOCUS

Long e Sound Practice with ie pattern

Sounds Like the letter e – *(ie)*
field
thief
piece
chief
brief
cookie
grief

Let continue with *long e sound* but with another sound letter pattern – **ie.**
The **ie** sound pattern just has one sound; just like the **ei** pattern that you practised before. This **ie** letter gives the long sound of **e**.

For example: fi**e**ld

Now practice saying the sound of words in the word-box above.

Here are some Pictures, write the words for them, using the word-box above.

....

(c) 2020 Roselle Thompson   *Phonic & Spelling Workbook 2*

....

EXTENSION

NOW READ THESE SENTENCES WITH ie SOUND WORDS AND THEN CIRCLE THEM. THEN WRITE THE SENTENCES.

1.	Let's go on the field to look for butterflies.
2.	Would you like a piece of cake?
3.	"Stop that thief, now!" cried the old man.
4.	The old Indian Chief is a very wise man.
5.	Mum baked some very yummy cookies for us.
6.	My teacher took us on a field trip to learn about ponds.
7.	The police will catch that thief, who is running away.
8.	Ben made his own shield and he coloured it pink, blue and silver.
9.	I will tell you a brief story, as I only have five minutes.
10.	Tom's old dog is dead, so he is full of grief right now.

CHALLENGE

Match the words that have ie sound pattern in them

field	bravery
measure	piece
chief	deceive
music	first
thief ——————→	cookie
bring	brief
green	grief
brief	achieve

WORD SEARCH: See if you can find these words:

BELIEVE, ACHIEVE, FIELD, BRIEF,
THIEF, GRIEF, PIECE, CHIEF, RELIEVE

B	R	I	E	F	A	G	B
A	F	E	I	H	C	R	E
P	I	E	C	E	H	I	L
M	E	R	C	A	I	E	I
O	L	T	H	I	E	F	E
C	D	E	I	F	V	B	V
D	R	E	L	I	E	V	E

Which is your favourite ie word? Write it here.................................

(c) 2020 Roselle Thompson *Phonic & Spelling Workbook 2*

REVIEWING ALL THE *LONG E* SOUND PATTERNS

NOW YOU NEED TO PRACTICE READING ALL THE *LONG E* SOUNDS
MIXED PRACTICE OF THE PATTERNS (e_e, ey, ee, ei, ea, ie, y)

1.	These are my new books and pens.
2.	Have you seen my key, I don't know where it is?
3.	My mum likes to drink tea.
4.	We drove into the city at the weekend.
5.	"Can you read a book?" asked John.
6.	I received lots of money on my birthday.
7.	"Let's bake some cookies for Nan," said my brother.
8.	It is very cold outside.
9.	I got a receipt when I paid for my food.
10.	All the boys are very happy because they won the game.
11.	"Can you complete this game for me," said Toby.
12.	My bike has two wheels.
13.	"Can I have a piece of cake, please? She asked.
14.	"I have never seen the Queen," said the little girl to her friend.
15.	The water in the pool is quite deep.
16.	We collected some worms in the field for our project.

How many sentences did you read correctly all by yourself?

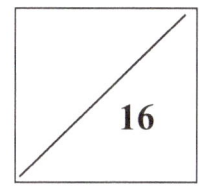

CHALLENGE

NOW TALK ABOUT THE DIFFERENT *LONG E* SOUND PATTERNS AGAIN. SEE IF YOU CAN WRITE THE WORDS FOR THESE PICTURES ALL BY YOURSELF

(c) 2020 Roselle Thompson   Phonic & Spelling Workbook 2

CERTIFICATE OF ACHIEVEMENT

LONG E PHONIC SOUND PATTERNS

This **Certificate** is presented to:

....for

successfully completing the entire LONG E SOUND PATTERNS as follows:

	I KNOW ALL MY e SOUND PATTERNS	
1.	e_e	✓
2.	ee	✓
3.	ey	✓
4.	ea	✓
5.	y	✓
6.	ei	✓
7.	ie	✓

Comment: ....

....

....

Teacher/Parent Signature: ....

Date: ....

High Frequency Words to help 7/8 year olds write stories

that	here	put	hair	add
there	when	help	more	after
their	where	play	house	fairy
they	out	help	more	sorry
then	what	open	near	money
this	put	made	hear	love
them	our	much	face	come
she	try	made	year	funny
her	have	nice	lady	coming
you	very	into	house	making
your	said	little	speak	count
with	were	near	fire	find
some	said	eyes	happy	father
want	nice	talk	first	doing
are	every	walk	sick	mother
saw	ever	story	home	brother
sister	by	never	baby	other
by	ever	baby	give	dinner
try	down	water	butter	supper
kind	again	water	table	going
new	itself	just	goes	work
does	next	some	please	could
would	tried	next	later	upon
once	please	anything	tea	door
drive	just	clock	only	girl
round	ground	found	thing	small
about	same	over	more	week
name	night	turn	dance	great
next	later	cousin	name	night
turn	next	later	cousin	whole
early	time	number	behind	nothing
key	use	better	many	try
why	who	hour	ask	which
speak	walk	trace	think	become
open	tomorrow	baby	tiny	where
upon	once	young	fairy	story
live	last	happily	after	upon
number	right	three	friend	moment

money	done	bright	stand	pretend
long	fight	pretty	person	close
join	start	five	easy	stay
today	upstairs	drink	sure	busy
such	follow	from	because	cannot
without	start	jump	beginning	something
tonight	football	away	plenty	quickly
think	noise	paper	finish	hurry
teacher	feel	under	silly	afraid
teach	few	black	forest	birthday
door	please	white	below	touch
children	even	chair	write	music
another	clever	smell	afraid	scream
smile	neat	throw	buy	weather
while	heard	slow	move	rainbow
wait	door	fast	use	please
body	child	old	blood	many
place	blame	wake	break	better
thank	air	close	steal	feel
cost	slow	open	should	world
lift	garden	blow	none	forget
itself	forget	join	hungry	town
seem	start	sound	sometimes	paper
find	own	grow	return	sugar
sleep	dream	easy	bottom	dark
suppose	happily	ever	after	huge
quick	inside	street	sudden	young
bedroom	outside	happen	weak	class
pain	care	fight	strong	ready
two	afraid	loud	beautiful	danger
one	down	down	grown	awful
few	return	turn	hurt	use
close	surprise	finish	soft	spring
scream	stuck	drop	stop	family
city	lady	notice	manage	someone
myself	night	outside	inside	village
splash	hope	burn	smoke	flew
throw	town	draw	blow	grew

No go on to Phonics & Spelling Workbook 2!

About the Author

Roselle Thompson B.A Hons, MPhil, FRSA, has over 30 years of experience in teaching and education development in the UK. In addition to her academic lecturing and writing, Roselle is also an Author, Poet, Playwright, Editor and Broadcaster, who has been creating, since 1994, intensive courses in a number of subjects; including English (language and literature), Verbal Reasoning and Public Speaking for children from as young as 5 years old, to GCSE Secondary and A level 6th Form. Roselle has Headed Education institutions from Nursery to Secondary levels and has also lectured at University. As a Broadcaster and International Speaker, her approach is therefore to make her significantly accumulated skills available to her students for their personal empowerment, development and life-long success.

BOOKS IN THE SERIES, BY THE SAME AUTHOR...............

- ### *ENGLISH GRAMMAR: A STUDENT'S COMPANION*

This book prepares children for the **11+ independent** and State **grammar schools** as well as the **Key Stage 2 SATs tests** and **Common Entrance** at 13 years. Although there are a variety of grammar books on the market, this book is based on over 27 years of the Author's techniques based on teaching, heading schools and rigorously tested exercises done in both school and tuition classrooms. The book contains a thorough preparation in grammar, and has valuable **exercises for all aspects of foundation English literacy development** to **secondary level** education and **beyond**. **The Book is divided into 6 sections with Learning Targets, Focus and Assessment indicators and 145 Test exercises, with Answers.** Each section includes work which **combines reading and writing skills to meet pupils' learning targets.**

- ### *VOCABULARY SKILLS FOR PRACTICAL LEARNING*

The Vocabulary book contains over **60 Units** and **60 Unit Tests** which can be used as lessons, **with a total of 600 vocabulary words.** Each Unit presents at least 10 vocabulary words which show their class or part of speech, together with their definition. This is followed by **60 gap-filling worksheet exercises** for you to complete, without looking at the meaning. Each gap-filling exercise helps students to see how these words are used in their contexts and tests the child's knowledge of them. Check out the **39 general knowledge challenges** set throughout the book as well as **16 interesting brain-teasing crossword puzzles!**

- ### *SPELLING & WORD POWER SKILLS*

The books in the **Spelling & Word-Power Series** cover **3 levels of practice**, arranged from **Starters** (which introduces the structure of words, sounds and rules), **Level 1** (expands knowledge of phonics and increases the level of structuring of words and rules which guide them), **Level 2** and **Level 3** (provides more challenges in exercises and rules that provides a structure within which the child is equipped with more advanced tools to learn, understand and spell at more advanced levels). Each level introduces spelling concepts, with explanation to help establish the rules which guide the approach to spelling techniques at each grade. **Rules** are identified and practice is given in exercises that test understanding. **Practice exercises** for you to complete, test your understanding of the rules applied. In this book, to help you spell correctly, there are spelling strategies that look at the certain aspects of the **sound, structure and spelling of words.**

- ### *MASTERING COMPREHENSION SKILLS*

This book provides a complete package of introduction, revision and practice comprehension passages to help you with preparation for the Key Stage 2 SATs tests and those preparing for the 11+ independent and state grammar school tests at 13 as well as preparation for GCSE English Language Paper 1. The passages cover work in Key Stage 2, 3, & 4 of the National Curriculum and beyond. The texts in this book have been carefully selected to be age-appropriate and cover a range of text types. The format of the questions replicates the SATs Reading and Comprehension tests to help your child become familiar with the format of the tests.

- ### *11+ ENGLISH PREPARATION TESTS FOR CEM EXAM*

. This book has been written to develop literacy and reasoning skills and is specifically aimed at:
  - ❖ Those taking the 11+ papers
  - ❖ Grammar school Entrance tests
  - ❖ Independent Secondary School entrance tests
  - ❖ Those considering taking Scholarship papers

Although the Practice tests are designed to reflect the style of the CEM tests, it also provides suitable preparation for all 11+ tests in general. This Book includes 5 Practice Tests with Answers.

www.ingramcontent.com/pod-product-compliance
Lightning Source LLC
Chambersburg PA
CBHW042016090526
44588CB00023B/2880